1662

March 26th. I had a pretty dinner for them, viz. a brace of stewed carps, six roasted chickens, and a jowl of salmon, hot, for the first course; a tanzy (*a pudding, named after the herb tansy which was used for making puddings*) and two neats' tongues, and cheese the second; and were very merry in the afternoon, talking and singing and piping upon the flageolette.

Samuel Pepys (1633–1703)

# STUART COOKERY

## Recipes & History

by
Peter Brears

with a Foreword by
Loyd Grossman OBE

ENGLISH HERITAGE

*Front cover:* Detail from *A Woman Gutting Fish in a Kitchen* by Gian Domenico Valentino

*Endpapers:* Bakers' tools illustrated in Randle Holme's *Academy of Armory*, 1688. 1. Meal shovel; 2. Kneading trough; 3. Dough scraper; 4. Brake; 5. Moulding table; 6. Dough knife; 7. Oven; 8. Gorse kindling on a pitchfork; 9. Peel; 10. Custard filler

Published by English Heritage, 23 Savile Row, London W1S 2ET

Copyright © English Heritage and Peter Brears
First published 1985
Revised edition 2004

ISBN 1 85074 872 1

Product code 50852

Edited by Susan Kelleher, Publishing, English Heritage, Kemble Drive, Swindon SN2 2GZ
Designed by Pauline Hull
Picture research by Elaine Willis
Brought to press by Andrew McLaren
Printed in England by CPI Bath

# CONTENTS

# FOREWORD

Would the pyramids have been built without the recently invented bread to efficiently feed the workforce? Food is a common denominator between us all, and a potent link with our ancestors, just as much as an ancient parish church or a listed house.

I am delighted to contribute a Foreword to English Heritage's series of historic cookery books, which neatly combine two of my passions – history and food. Most of us no longer have to catch or grow our own food before eating it, but the continuing daily need for sustenance still powerfully links us with our earliest forebears. We may not like the thought of Roman fish sauce made from fermented entrails (until we next add oyster sauce to a Chinese beef dish), but we can only sigh with recognition at a Jacobean wife's exhortation to 'let yor butter bee scalding hott in yor pan' before pouring in the beaten eggs for an omelette. The Roman penchant for dormice cooked in milk doesn't resonate with us now, but a dish of pears in red wine features at modern dinner parties just as it did in medieval times.

Food and cooking have inevitably changed down the centuries, as modern cookers have supplanted open hearths, and increased wealth and speedy transport have opened up modern tastes and palates to the widest range of ingredients and cuisines. But it's worth remembering that it was the Romans who gave us onions, sugar was an expensive luxury in the 16th century as was tea in the 17th, the tomato only became popular in Europe in the 19th century and even in the 1950s avocados and red peppers were still exotic foreign imports.

I urge you to experiment with the recipes in these books which cover over 2,000 years, and hope you enjoy, as I have, all that is sometimes strange and often familiar about the taste of times past.

**Loyd Grossman** OBE
Former Commissioner of English Heritage
Chairman of the Campaign for Museums

# INTRODUCTION

The 17th century was a period of tremendous upheaval and change in this country – a period in which virtually every aspect of our national and domestic life was transformed as England cast off many of her medieval traditions to emerge as a new, forward-looking state. As a result of the dissolution of the monasteries in the 1530s, vast areas of land and previously untapped economic resources had passed into lay hands. As they were enthusiastically developed over the succeeding century, their growing productivity financed the rise of what was to be a new, prosperous and influential class – the landed gentry.

In an age when the sovereign sturdily maintained his Divine Right to govern as he wished, it was impossible for the gentry to obtain the political power they now sought. The resulting friction between these opposing views flared up into the Civil War that terminated in the execution of Charles I in 1649. After just a decade of puritanical Commonwealth government, England returned to monarchy with Charles II in 1660. However, it was now a

*Opposite:* Attractive blue-painted pottery became fashionable in the 17th century

constitutional monarchy that recognised the right of Parliament to play a leading role in managing the country's affairs.

These upheavals had a considerable effect on domestic life. From the early 1600s, the increasing affluence of the gentry had enabled them to spend much more on recreation, travel and luxury goods. Instead of living throughout the year on their quiet estates, they now spent long periods in the towns, visits to London allowing them to acquire all manner of social graces. Here they might participate in advantageous parliamentary, commercial or legal business, perhaps take fencing or dancing lessons, use the services of fine tailors and wig-makers, or enjoy excursions to the theatre, musical events, great houses, or the court. In the 1620s, proclamations ordered the gentry to return to their estates to prevent the neglect of public duties, avoidance of tax and the heavy expenditure on foreign luxuries and expensive foods. These were largely ignored, however, and lavish entertainment flourished during the London season, as the city continued to develop as the finest food market in the kingdom.

Up to this time the fare of the country gentleman had been relatively plain and simple, largely based on home-produced meat, game and grain, roasted, boiled or baked as required. Plenty had been preferred to variety, but now there was an increasing demand for new delicacies, with new flavours and new methods of cookery. As in all new aspects of social life, the royal household set the required standards of culinary taste, drawing both on its own centuries-old traditions and on new developments from France. Dishes which appeared at court would be imitated in lesser households, and thus proceed on down the social scale, as the recipes were probably passed on at dinner or supper parties. At these functions the ladies would also exchange recipes for their own specialities, together with those

Dressed in the height of fashion, a gentleman enjoys a summer picnic

# THE
# ENGLISH
## House-Wife,

### CONTAING

The inward and outward Vertues which
ought to be in a Compleat WOMAN.

As her Skill in *Physick*, *Chirurgery*, *Cookery*, *Extraction of Oyls*,
*Banqueting stuff*, *Ordering of great Feasts*, *Preserving of all sort of
Wines*, *conceited Secrets*, *Distillations*, *Perfumes*, *Ordering of Wool*,
*Hemp*, *Flax*: Making *Cloth* and *Dying*; The knowledge of
*Dayries*: Office of *Malting*; of *Oats*, their excellent uses in Fa-
milies: Of *Brewing*, *Baking*, and all other things belonging to an
Houshold.

A *Work* generally approved, and now the
Eighth time much Augmented, Purged, and made most
profitable and necessary for all men, and the general good
of this NATION.

By *G. Markham.*

*LONDON,*
Printed for *George Sawbridge*, at the Sign of the *Bible* on
*Ludgate Hill.* 1675.

culled from the ever-increasing range of recipe books. Between 1600 and 1700 a new volume appeared almost every other year, the most popular of these often running into a number of editions. With titles such as *The English House-Wife; The Accomplisht Lady's Delight*, or *The Genteel House-Keeper's Pastime*, they appear to have been primarily intended for use in prosperous families, where the lady of the house was responsible for all aspects of housekeeping. Many of the recipes were individually attributed to the royal kitchens, or to ladies of the

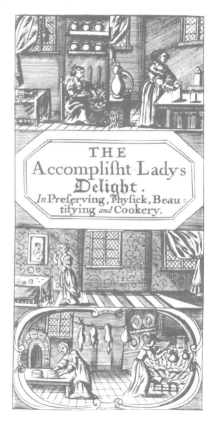

*Right:* The frontispiece of *The Accomplisht Lady's Delight* of 1675 shows ladies busily preserving, distilling, making cosmetics and working in the kitchen

*Opposite:* Title page, *The English House-Wife*, 1675

> 'The receipts
> of cookery
> are swelled
> to a volume;
> but a good
> stomach excels
> them all.'
>
> William Penn (1644–1718)

court, which presumably gave them a certain socially prestigious cachet. These volumes contained many items from overseas, such as 'a Persian Dish', 'a Turkish Dish', 'a Portugal Dish', or even 'an Outlandish Dish', but France provided the most fertile source of the new recipes. In the late 16th century Sir Hugh Platt had published some 'after the French fashion', while John Murrell's *New Booke of Cookerie* of 1617 was 'all set forth according to the now new English and French Fashion'. F. P. de La Varenne's *Cuisinier françois*, published in Paris in 1651, was to have the greatest influence, particularly after it was 'English'd by J.G.D.' and appeared as *The French Cook* in London in 1653. It included recipes for hash, and for dishes both 'a la daube' and 'a la mode'. By 1688 cooks' glossaries included a wide range of newly introduced French terms, including:

'*A-la-Sauces* Sauce made after the French Almaigne or German fashion.

*A-la-Doode* is a French way of ordering any large Fowl or Leg of Mutton.

*A-la-Mode way* is the new, or French way of dressing all manner of boiled or baked Meat.

*Bouillon* is a kind of Broth or boiled meat made of several things.

*Hash* is a Dishmeat made of any kind of flesh minced or in Gobbets stewed in strong broth with spices, and served up in a Dish with Sippets: to Hash is to stew any Meat that is cold. The French call it Hach or Hachee.

*Hautgoust* a thing that hath an high taste, viz. a Ho-goo.

*Salmagundi* an Italian dish, [actually from France] made of cold turkey and other Ingredients.'

Although a number of new dishes were introduced from other European countries such as Italy's macaroni, vermicelli and 'tortelleti', and Spain's 'olla podrida' (an amazing variety of stewed meats and vegetables, anglicised as 'hotch-potch'), the French influence was predominant. Even so, it did not overwhelm the native English taste for good, plain cooking. Many still preferred substantial, solid,

The coffee houses which developed in cities across the country soon became fashionable places to meet, drink – and smoke. The delights of tobacco had been discovered and pipe smoking became widespread among both men and women. It was claimed that smoking was good for the health using the argument that as mens' brains were cold and moist anything hot and dry must benefit them! However, a number of people, including the

king, were opposed to smoking. In 1604 James I attacked smoking in his famous pamphlet *Counterblast to Tobacco*. He effectively proved that all claims that smoking was healthy were unfounded, and denounced the habit as barbarous and playing into the hands of England's enemies (ie the Spanish). He summed up smoking as 'a custom loathsome to the eye, hateful to the nose, harmful to the brain, dangerous to the lungs, and in the black stinking fume thereof nearest resembling the horrible Stygian smoke of the pit that is bottomless'.

wholesome roast and boiled meats, to the highly priced Frenchified 'Hogg-podg Dish-meats, neither pleasing to the Pallet, or of credit to the Masters ... But let Cooks study new Dish-meats and work out their Brains, when they have done all they can, there are but four sorts of Meat which they can properly, and with safety, work upon, viz. Flesh of Beasts, Flesh of Fowle, Flesh of Fish and Field Fruits; and these again are according to their kinds either Stewed, Boiled, Parboiled, Fryed, Broiled, Roasted, Baked, Hashed, Pickled, Souced, or made into Sweet-Meats. Nil Ultra.'

The recipes which follow have been chosen to demonstrate a typical range of 17th-century dishes, and to give some impression of their diverse flavours. They include some of the newly introduced varieties of pudding and bakery, in addition to contemporary versions of well-established foods.

First and second courses for a meal may be made up from a combination of any of the meat dishes with a pudding and either hot or cold roasts; while the various sweets, cakes and biscuits, with fresh fruit and cheese, can form a banquet or third course. As an alternative, any of the recipes can be used individually as part of an otherwise modern meal.

*Recipes*

# DIET BREAD

*The receypte of the Dyett bread: Take halfe a pecke of fyne Wheaten Flower, three handfull of sage shredd small, An ounce and a halfe of ordinary Fennell seede lightly bruised, strawe the sage and the Fennell seede amongst the Flower, and so with barme kneade and bake ytt as you do other breade, and eate ytt nott until ytt be a day old.*

**400 g (14 oz) plain flour**
**30 ml (2 tbls) dried sage**
**15 g ($^1/_2$ oz) fennel seed, bruised**
**15 g ($^1/_2$ oz) dried yeast mixed**
**with 5 ml (1 tsp) sugar and**
**275 ml ($^1/_2$ pt) warm water**

Mix the dry ingredients in a warm bowl, make a well in the centre and work in the liquid. Knead, and then leave to rise in a warm place for 1 hour. Knead the dough on a floured board, shape into a round cob or a number of small cakes, and allow to prove for 15 minutes before baking at gas mark 8, 230°C (450°F) for 15 minutes, and then for a further 40 minutes at gas mark 6, 200°C (400°F). This bread has a delicate aniseed flavour, and makes an interesting accompaniment to soups, fish or cheese.

A Temple Newsam recipe quoted in
*The Gentlewoman's Kitchen*

*Opposite:* Fennel and parsley – popular herbs used in a variety of recipes

# SCOTCH COLLOPS

*To Make Scotch Collops: R. a legge of Mutton, cutt itt in round pieces as broad as you can, & the thickness of a thin halfe-crowne, fry them in sweet butter very browne, but not too hard, then take four or five spoonfull of vinegar, an onion slit, halfe a nuttmegge grated, Lemon-pill, an Anchovee, a little horseradish, & oysters if you have them, putt all into the Frying-pan together with the meat, & a quarter of a pound of butter beaten thick, tosse them in the Pan a while over the fire, but do not let them boyle, then heat your dish, rubb it with Shallot or garlick, & send them upp quick.*

**450 g (I lb) lean lamb or mutton**
**175 g (6 oz) butter**
**75 ml (5 tbls) claret**
**30 ml (2 tbls) vinegar**
**I onion**
**2 anchovy fillets**
**15 ml (I tbls) horseradish sauce**
**I garlic clove**

Thinly slice the meat, and stir fry gently with half the butter for 5–10 minutes until browned. Remove from the heat, and add all the remaining ingredients, except for the garlic. Heat gently for a few minutes, stirring the pan continuously, until almost at boiling point. Slice the garlic, and rub it around the inside of the serving dish before pouring in the collops. Serve immediately. This is an excellent way of making a rich and full-flavoured meat dish in a very short time.

*The Savile Recipe Book*, 1683, quoted in
*The Gentlewoman's Kitchen*

Early 17th-century woodcut of a butcher

# BOILED BREAST OF MUTTON

*First boyle him in water and salte,*
*then take halfe a pinte of whight wine*
*vineger, and as much of the broth yor*
*muton was boyled in, large mace,*
*and some suger a handfull of parsley,*
*time, and sweete marierom, the yelkes*
*of fower hard egges and a little of the*
*rine of an oringe, yor herbes egges and*
*oringe rinde must bee chopped smale*
*and boyled in your broath, when yt is*
*well boyled lay yor muten on sippetts*
*in a dish, and put a good peece of*
*sweete Buter into yor broath and so*
*powre yt on yor muton, On the topp*
*lay sliced Limondes and capers but*
*yor Capers must bee layed in warme*
*water the space of a quarter of an*
*hower ere you lay them on yor meate.*

**900 g (2lb) breast of lamb**
**15 ml (1 tbls) white wine vinegar**

**handful of parsley, thyme and**
 **marjoram, chopped**
**rind of ¹/2 an orange**
**4 egg yolks, hard-boiled**

To serve:
**capers**
**2 lemons, sliced**

Chop the breast of lamb into sections
and remove as much of the fat as
possible. Simmer in enough salted
water to cover (probably around 575 ml
1 pt) in a lidded pan for 1–1¹/2 hours.
Remove the meat to a very hot dish
and keep warm. Add the white wine
vinegar to the liquor in the pan and
reduce if necessary by fast boiling to
about 275 ml (¹/2 pt). Simmer for a few
minutes. Pound the herbs with the egg
yolks and stir in the broth with a

seasoning of sugar, mace (or nutmeg) and the orange rind. If using an ordinary sweet orange, add a squeeze of lemon juice. More salt can be added if necessary. Reheat the sauce, which will be quite thick, with a knob of butter, and pour it over the meat. Serve, topped with capers previously plumped in hot water and slices of lemon.

*Elinor Fettiplace's Receipt Book*

The chopped whites of a couple of the eggs can also be used to decorate the meat before serving.

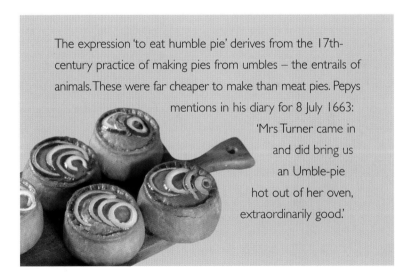

The expression 'to eat humble pie' derives from the 17th-century practice of making pies from umbles – the entrails of animals. These were far cheaper to make than meat pies. Pepys mentions in his diary for 8 July 1663: 'Mrs Turner came in and did bring us an Umble-pie hot out of her oven, extraordinarily good.'

# DUTCH PUDDING

*Take a pound and a halfe of Fresh Beef, all lean, take a pound and a quarter of Beef Suet, sliced both very small, then take a halfpenny stale Loaf and grate it, a handfull of Sage and a little Winter Savory, a little Time, shred these very small; take four Eggs, half a pint of Cream, a few Cloves, Nutmegs, Mace and Pepper, finely beaten, mingle them all together very well, with a little Salt; roll it all up together in a green Colwort Leaf, and then tye it up hard in a Linnen-Cloth, garnish your Dish with grated bread and serve it up with mustard in Sawcers.*

**350 g (12 oz) coarsely minced lean beef**
**225 g (8 oz) suet**
**100 g (4 oz) dry breadcrumbs**
**10 ml (2 tsps) dried sage**
**5 ml (1 tsp) dried savory**
**5 ml (1 tsp) dried thyme**
**2 eggs**
**1.5 ml ('/4 tsp) ground cloves**
**1.5 ml ('/4 tsp) grated nutmeg**
**1.5 ml ('/4 tsp) ground mace**
**1.5 ml ('/4 tsp) pepper**
**10 ml (2 tsps) salt**
**1–2 large cabbage leaves**

To serve:
**fresh breadcrumbs**
**freshly made English mustard**

Mix all the ingredients together and form into a round ball. Wrap in a large cabbage leaf or 2 smaller ones, and tie up tightly in a linen cloth. Plunge into boiling water and simmer for 2 hours. To serve, turn out of the cloth on to a bed of fresh breadcrumbs, accompanied by a saucer of English mustard. The dish looks just like a cabbage at this stage, but may be carved with ease.

Elizabeth Cromwell: *The Court and Kitchen of Mrs Elizabeth Commonly called Joan Cromwell*

This dish is also delicious served with a fruit sauce made from blackberries.

# BRAWN

*To bake Brawne: Take two Buttocks...
take Lard, cut it in pieces as big as
your little finger, and season it very
well with Pepper, Cloves, Mace,
Nutmeg, and Salt, put each of them
into an earthen Pot, put in a pint of
Claret-wine, a pound of Mutton Suet.
So close it with paste, let the Oven
be well heated, and so bake them...*

**900 g – 1.4 kg (2–3lb) joint of pork**
**350 ml (1/2 bottle) claret**
**50 g (2 oz) suet**
**10 ml (2 tsps) salt**
**2.5 ml (1/2 tsp) ground mace**
**1.5 ml (1/4 tsp) pepper**
**1.5 ml (1/4 tsp) ground cloves**
**1.5 ml (1/4 tsp) grated nutmeg**

Shortcrust pastry made with:
**100 g (4 oz) plain flour**
**50 g (2 oz) lard**

Trim any fat or rind from the joint, and
cut into strips. Truss the joint tightly, place
in a deep casserole, then add the strips
of fat and the remaining ingredients
except for the pastry. Roll out the pastry,
and use it to cover the casserole,
carefully sealing the edges. Bake at gas
mark 4, 180°C (350°F) for 2 1/2 hours,
then leave in a cool place overnight.
Remove the crust, lift out the joint,
wipe clean, and carve as required. The
remaining stock can be used to provide
a highly flavoured basis for soups etc.

Rebecca Price: *The Compleat Cook*

# CHICKEN CULLIS

*To make a cullis as white as snowe
and in the nature of gelly: Take a
cocke, scalde, wash and draw him
clene, seeth it in white wine or rhenish
wine, skum it cleane, clarifie the broth
after it is strained, then take a pinte of
thicke & sweet creame, straine that to
your clarified broth, and your broth
will become exceeding faire and white;
then take powdred ginger, fine white
sugar and Rosewater, seething your
cullis when you season it, to make it
take the colour the better.*

**1 chicken**
**850 ml (1¹/₂ pt) white wine**
**1 egg white, lightly beaten**
**575 ml (1 pt) single cream**
**2.5 ml (¹/₂ tsp) ground ginger**
**30 ml (2 tbls) sugar**
**15 ml (1 tbls) rosewater**

Simmer the chicken in the wine until tender – about 45–50 minutes. Remove the chicken from the pan and keep it hot. Beat the egg white into the stock and continue to whisk over a moderate heat until it comes to the boil. Stop whisking immediately and allow the liquid to rise to the top of the pan before removing it from the heat for a few minutes to allow the fine particles to form a soft curd with the egg white. Pour the liquid through a fine cloth into a clean pan, place on a gentle heat, and stir slowly while pouring in the cream. Heat the cullis almost to boiling point, stirring continuously, and finally add the ginger, sugar and rosewater just before serving.

The cullis may be poured over the chicken resting on crustless cubes of white bread, in a deep dish. Alternatively, it can be served separately as a soup.

Sir Hugh Platt: *Delightes for Ladies*

# SALAD

For the salad:

**young leaves of lettuce, sorrel,
mustard, cress, dandelion,
spinach, radishes**

**225 g (8 oz) capers**

**12 dates, sliced lengthways**

**50 g (2 oz) raisins**

**50 g (2 oz) currants**

**50 g (2 oz) blanched almonds**

**6 figs, sliced**

**6 mandarin oranges, peeled and
divided into segments**

For the decoration:

**5 small branches of rosemary**

**4 lemons**

**225 g (8 oz) fresh or glacé
cherries**

**6 hard-boiled eggs**

Mix the contents of the salad together
(reserving half the capers, dates,
almonds and oranges for decoration)
and spread evenly across a wide
shallow dish. Spike each branch of
rosemary into the pointed end of five
half-lemons, and hang with the cherries
before placing one in the centre of the
salad, and the remaining four
equidistant around it. Prick 4 half-eggs
with the reserved almonds and dates,
both sliced lengthways, and place these
between the four half-lemons. Quarter
the remaining eggs, and alternate with
slices of lemon just within the brim of
the dish. Then decorate the brim with
alternating orange segments and small
piles of capers.

*The Second Book of Cookery*

# PICKLED MUSHROOMS

*Take your Buttons, clean ym with a spunge & put ym in cold water as you clean ym, then put ym dry in a stewpan & shake a handfull of salt over ym, yn stew ym in their own liquor till they are a little tender; then strain ym from ye liquor & put ym upon a cloath to dry till they are quite cold. Make your Pickle before you do your Mushrooms, yt may be quite cold before you put ym in. The Pickle must be made with White-Wine, White-Pepper, quarter'd Nutmeg, a Blade of Mace, & a Race of ginger.*

**450 g (1 lb) button mushrooms**
**190 ml (¹/₃ pt) white wine**
**6 white peppercorns**
**¹/₂ a nutmeg**
**5 ml (1 tsp) salt**

**blade of mace**
**2 cm (1 in) piece of root ginger**

Peel and slice the root ginger and put in a small saucepan with the wine, peppercorns, nutmeg and mace and simmer, with the saucepan lid on, for 10 minutes. Add a few spoonfuls of water if the liquid evaporates too quickly. Leave to cool.

Wipe the mushrooms clean and put them, whole, in a large, thick-bottomed saucepan with a heaped teaspoon of salt, and heat gently, shaking and stirring with a wooden spoon, especially at first before the juices begin to flow. Keep the lid on between stirs. It will only take about 10 minutes until they are tender. Watch them constantly and try to take them off at exactly the right moment when there will be little or no liquor to strain off. When they are cold, pot them in sterilised and tightly sealed jars if they are for pickling. If they are to be eaten straight away, pour the marinade straight on the mushrooms in their pan as soon as they are done. Decant into a dish and leave, covered, for a few hours to develop their flavour. Serve with chopped parsley and fresh bread – or sippets.

*Elinor Fettiplace's Receipt Book*

## 1662

June 26th. Up and took physique, but such as to go abroad with, only to loosen me, for I am bound. So to the office, and there all the morning sitting till noon, and then took Commissioner Pett home to dinner with me, where my stomach was turned when my sturgeon came to table, upon which I saw very many little worms creeping, which I suppose was through the staleness of the pickle.

Samuel Pepys (1633–1703)

# ALE-BASED APPLE FRITTERS

*Take good ale, make yt bloud warme,*
*put to yt some fine wheatne flower,*
*the yelkes of 4 or 5 egges, some Cloves,*
*mace and smale quantity of ginger,*
*with some salte, and a qter of a*
*pound of beefe suett shred very smale,*
*temper yt all well together, then pare*
*yor apples, Cut out the Cores & slice*
*them round into yor batter, and bake*
*them in beife Lard as other fritures.*

**275 ml (¹/2 pt) light ale**
**225 g (8 oz) plain flour**
**5 ml (I tsp) ginger**
**2 or 3 ground cloves**
**pinch of powdered mace**
**4 or 5 egg yolks**
**100 g (4 oz) shredded beef suet**
**1.4 kg (3 lb) sweet eating apples**
  **(pippins)**

Mix the spices into the flour and then make up a batter with the seasoned flour, ale, eggs and suet, making sure it is not too thin. Beat it well and leave to stand for an hour or so. Meanwhile, slice the apples into rings and then drop them into the batter. Heat butter, lard or pure beef dripping in a large frying pan and, when very hot, put in the apple rings. Fry over a moderate heat for a few minutes each side, then remove carefully and drain on kitchen paper. Dust with sugar and spices and serve, adding more sugar, ginger and cinnamon to taste.

*Elinor Fettiplace's Receipt Book*

Pepys loved these fritters and enjoyed them at different houses on most Shrove Tuesdays.

'Is not
old wine
wholesomest, old
pippins toothsomest,
old wood burns brightest,
old linen wash whitest?
Old soldiers, sweetheart,
are surest, and old lovers are
soundest.'

John Webster (1580?–1633), *Westward Hoe*

# QUAKING PUDDING

*To make a quaking Pudding: Take a pint and somewhat more of thick Cream, ten Eggs, put the whites of three, beat them very well with two spoonfuls of Rosewater: mingle with your cream three spoonfuls of fine flour: mingle it so well, that there be no lumps in it, put it altogether, and season it according to your Taste: butter a Cloth very well, and let it be thick that it may not run out, and let it boyl for half an hour as fast as you can, then take it up and make Sauce with butter, Rosewater and sugar, and serve it up.*

**4 egg yolks**
**2 egg whites**
**275 ml (¹/₂ pt) double cream**
**25 ml (1 ¹/₂ tbls) flour**
**15 ml (1 tbls) rosewater**

For the sauce:
**30 ml (2 tbls) rosewater**
**30 ml (2 tbls) sugar**
**50 g (2 oz) butter**
**30 ml (2 tbls) water**

Beat the egg yolks and whites into the cream, then beat in the flour and rosewater to form a thick batter. Rub a piece of butter into a thick pudding cloth to help it retain the batter. Support the cloth in a 575 ml (1 pt) basin, pour in the batter, tie the cloth securely, and plunge the pudding into a pan of boiling water. Simmer for 30 minutes, then remove from the pan and swiftly plunge into cold water. Turn the pudding out on to a warm plate. Make the sauce by melting the ingredients together, stirring constantly, and pour over the pudding.

Rebecca Price: *The Compleat Cook*

# DEVONSHIRE WHITE POT

*Take a pint of Cream and strain four Eggs into it, and put a little salt and a little sliced Nutmeg, and season it with sugar somewhat sweet, then take almost a penny Loaf of fine bread sliced very thin, and put it into a dish that will hold it, the Cream and the Eggs being put to it, then take a handfull of Raisins of the Sun being boiled, and a little sweet Butter, so bake it.*

**50 g (2 oz) raisins**
**450 g (1 lb) white bread, crusts removed and thinly sliced**
**25 g (1 oz) butter**
**3 eggs**

**575 ml (1 pt) single cream**
**1.5 ml ('/4 tsp) grated nutmeg**
**1.5 ml ('/4 tsp) salt**
**75 g (3 oz) sugar**

Soak the raisins in hot water for 10 minutes. Line a 1.1 litre (2 pt) ovenproof dish with some of the bread. Put the remainder in the centre of the dish, mixing in the raisins and knobs of the butter. Beat the eggs with the cream and stir in the nutmeg, salt and sugar. Pour over the bread, and allow it to stand for 15 minutes. Bake at gas mark 4, 180°C (350°F) for 40–50 minutes.

Rebecca Price: *The Compleat Cook*

# COURT SOPS (CINNAMON TOAST)

*Take ale and sugar and nutmeg and boile it together, and then have manchet cut like tostes and tost them browne, and then put them in the ale one by another without breaking of them, then boile it till the sops bee drie, then put some butter in it, and straw some sugar and nutmeg on it, and so serve it when it is somewhat cold.*

**275 ml ('/2 pt) brown ale**
**15 ml (I tbls) sugar**
**nutmeg to taste**
**cinnamon to taste**
**4 slices of thick white bread**

Heat the ale, sugar and nutmeg, stirring until the sugar has dissolved. Toast the bread as slowly as possible and then lay the slices in a baking dish. Pour over the ale (it would be at least 10 mm ('/2 in) deep for the bread to soak up), and leave the dish in a slow oven or any other warm place for about 10 minutes, but it can be left much longer. Add more liquid if necessary and serve the sops buttered with a sprinkling of cinnamon, and more sugar and nutmeg if necessary.

*Elinor Fettiplace's Receipt Book*

The beauty of this dish is that it can be left almost indefinitely, toasting on top and steeping below.

# KNOT BISCUITS

*To make Knotts or Gumballs: Take*
*12 Yolkes of Eggs, & 5 Whites, a*
*pound of searced Sugar, half a*
*pound of Butter washed in Rose*
*Water, 3 quarters of an ounce of*
*Mace finely beaten, a little Salt*
*dissolved in Rose Water, half an*
*ounce of Caroway-seeds, Mingle all*
*theise together with as much Flower*
*as will work it up in paste, & soe*
*make it Knotts or Rings or What*
*fashion you please. Bake them as*
*Bisket-bread, put upon Pye-plates.*

**40 g (1½ oz) butter**
**15 ml (1 tbls) rosewater**
**100 g (4 oz) sugar**

**2 eggs, beaten**
**5 ml (1 tsp) ground mace**
**5 ml (1 tsp) aniseed**
**5 ml (1 tsp) caraway seed**
**225 g (8 oz) flour**

Beat the butter with the rosewater,
then cream with the sugar. Mix in the
beaten eggs and spices, then work in
the flour to make it a stiff dough. Make
into long rolls about 5 mm (¼ in) in
diameter, and form into knots, rings or
plaited strips before baking on lightly
greased baking sheets for 15–20
minutes at gas mark 4, 180°C (350°F).

Henry Fairfax: *Arcana Fairfaxiana*

# MARZIPAN BACON

*To make Collops like Bacon of Marchpane: Take some of your Marchpane Paste and work it in red Saunders till it be red: then rowl a broad sheet of white Paste, and a sheet of red Paste, three of the white, and four of the red, and so one upon another in mingled sorts, every red between, then cut it overthwart, till it look like Collops of Bacon, then dry it.*

**225 g (8 oz) ground almonds**
**100 g (4 oz) caster sugar**
**30 ml (2 tbls) rosewater**
**red food colouring**
**cornflour or icing sugar for dusting**

Beat the almonds and sugar with the rosewater to form a stiff paste. Divide in two, and knead a few drops of the red food colour into one half. Using either cornflour or icing sugar to dust the paste, roll out half the white mixture into a rectangle about 10 mm ($^{1}/_{2}$ in) in thickness, and the remainder into three thinner rectangles of the same size. Divide the red paste into four, and roll each piece out into similar rectangles. Starting with the thick white slab ('the fat'), build up alternate red and white layers to form a piece of 'streaky bacon', from which thin slices or 'collops' can then be cut and allowed to dry.

W.M.: *The Compleat Cook and Queen's Delight*, 1671 edition

## SHROPSHIRE CAKES

*To make a Shropshire cake: Take two pound of dryed flour after it has been searced fine, one pound of good sugar dried and searced, also a little beaten sinamon or some nottmegg greeted and steeped in rose water; so straine two eggs, whites and all, not beaten to it, as much unmelted butter as will work it to a paste: so mould it & roule it into longe rouses, and cutt off as much at a time as will make a cake, two ounces is enough for one cake: then roule it in a ball between your hands; so flat it on a little white paper cut for a cake, and with your hand beat it about as big as a cheese trancher and a little thicker than a past board: then prick them with a comb not too deep in squares like diamons and prick the cake in every diamon to the bottom; so take them in an oven not too hot: when they rise up white let them soake a little, then draw. If the sugar be dry enough you need not dry it but searce it: you must brake in your eggs after you have wroat in some of your butter into your flower: prick and mark them when they are cold: this quantity will make a dozen and two or three, which is enough for my own at a time: take off the paper when they are cold.*

**225 g (8 oz) butter**
**450 g (1 lb) flour**
**225 g (8 oz) caster sugar**
**1.5 ml (¼ tsp) grated nutmeg**
**1 egg**
**5 ml (1 tsp) rosewater**

Rub the butter into the dry ingredients, then work in the egg and rosewater to form a very stiff dough. Cut off lumps of dough, and work into 5 mm (¼ in) thick cakes, 10 cm (4 in) in diameter. Using a comb, mark the top surface into diamonds, cutting half-way through the cake, then use a broad skewer to prick all the way through the centre of each diamond. Transfer to baking sheets, and bake for 20 minutes as gas mark 4, 180°C (350°F). Remove from the sheets with a metal spatula, and place on a wire tray to cool.

Madam Susanne Avery: *A Plain Plantain*

'It was a common saying among the Puritans, "Brown bread and the Gospel is good fare".'

Matthew Henry (1662–1714), *Commentaries*

# SPICE CAKE

*To make an Extraordinary Good
Cake: Take half a bushel of the best
flour you can get, very finely searced,
and lay it on a large pastry board,
make a hole in the middle thereof, put
to it three pounds of the best butter
you can get; with 14 pounds of
currants finely picked and rubbed,
three quarts of good new thick cream,
2 pounds of fine sugar beaten, 3 pints
of new ale barm or yeast, 4 ounces of
cinnamon beaten fine and searced,
also an ounce of beaten ginger,
2 ounces of nutmegs beaten fine and
searced; put all these material together,
and work them up to an indifferent
stiff paste. Keep it warm till the oven
be hot, then make it up and bake it,
being baked an hour and a half ice it,
then take 4 pounds of double refined
sugar, beat it and searce it, and put it*

*in a clean scowered skillet the quantity
of a gallon, and boil it to a candy
height with a little rosewater, then
draw the cake, run it all over, and set
it in the oven till it be candied.*

**75 g (3 oz) butter**
**450 g (1 lb) plain flour**
**350 g (12 oz) currants**
**50 g (2 oz) sugar**
**2.5 ml ('/2 tsp) ground cinnamon**
**2.5 ml ('/2 tsp) ground ginger**
**1.5 ml ('/4 tsp) grated nutmeg**
**275 ml ('/2 pt) cream**
**15 g ('/2 oz) dried yeast mixed
with 5 ml (1 tsp) sugar and
150 ml ('/4 pt) warm water**

For the glazing:
**15 ml (1 tbls) sugar**
**15 ml (1 tbls) rosewater**

Rub the butter into the flour, add the remainder of the dry ingredients, and mix in the cream and yeast to form a soft dough. Leave to rise in a warm place for about 1 hour, when it will have doubled in size, then knead and place in a greased 20 cm (8 in) cake tin. Leave to prove for 20 minutes, then bake at gas mark 7, 220°C (425°F) for 20 minutes, then for 1 hour at gas mark 5, 190°C (375°F). Melt the sugar in the rosewater over a low heat, and brush this glaze over the cake immediately after removing it from the oven.

Robert May: *The Accomplisht Cook*

'Cherry ripe, ripe, ripe, I cry,
Full and fair ones – come and buy!
If so be you ask me where
They do grow, I answer, There,
Where my Julia's lip do smile –
That's the land, or cherry-isle.'

Robert Herrick (1591-1674), *Cherry Ripe*

# GINGERBREAD

*To make Gingerbread: Take three stale Manchets and grate them, drie them, and sift them through a fine sieve, then adde unto them one ounce of ginger being beaten, and as much Cinamon, one ounce of liquorice and aniseedes being beaten together and searced, halfe a pound of sugar, then boile all these together in a posnet, with a quart of claret wine till they come to a stiff paste with often stirring of it; and when it is stiffe, mold it on a table and so drive it thin, and print it in your moldes: dust your moldes with Cinamon, Ginger and liquorice, being mixed together in fine powder. This is your gingerbread used at the Court, and in all gentlemens houses at festival times. It is othewise called drie Leach.*

**225 g (8 oz) fresh white breadcrumbs**
**5 ml (1 tsp) ground ginger**
**5 ml (1 tsp) cinnamon**
**5 ml (1 tsp) aniseed**
**5 ml (1 tsp) ground liquorice (if available)**
**25 g (1 oz) sugar**
**150 ml (¼ pt) claret**

Dry the breadcrumbs under the grill or in the oven (but without browning), and add to the remaining ingredients in a saucepan. Using a wooden spoon, work the mixture over a gentle heat until it forms a stiff dough. Turn the dough out on to a wooden board dusted with ground ginger and cinnamon and roll it out to about 5 mm (¼ in) in thickness. It may then

46

be impressed with a small stamp, a 2.5 cm (1 in) diameter butter print being ideal for this purpose, and cut into small circles using a pastry cutter. If antique gingerbread moulds are available, then they should be dusted with the ground spices before the slab of dough is firmly impressed into their designs. Then, after the surplus has been trimmed off with a knife, the gingerbread can be removed by inverting the moulds, and gently knocking their edges down on to the table.

Sir Hugh Platt: *Delightes for Ladies*

Like most early gingerbreads, this version releases its flavours gradually, the gentle aniseed being slowly overwhelmed by the fiery ginger.

'If you are not feeling well, if you have not slept, chocolate will revive you. But you have no chocolate! I think of that again and again! My dear, how will you ever manage?'

Marquise de Sévigné (French writer and lady of fashion) February 11, 1677

# SYLLABUS

*My Lady Middlesex makes
Syllabubs for little Glasses with
spouts, thus Take 3 pints of sweet
Cream, one of quick white wine (or
Rhenish), and a good wine glassful
(better the ¹/4 of a pint) of sack; mingle
them with about three quarters of a
pound of fine Sugar in Powder. Beat
all these together with a whisk, till all
appeareth converted into froth. Then
pour it into your little Syllabub-
glasses, and let them stand all night.
The next day the curd will be thick
and firm above, and the drink clear
under it. I conceive it may do well, to
put into each glass (when you pour
your liquor into it) a sprig of
Rosemary a little bruised, or a little
Lemon-peel, or some such thing to
quicken the taste … or Nutmegs, or
Mace, or Cloves, a very little.*

**575 ml (1 pt) double cream**
**200 ml (7 fl oz) Rhenish white**
**wine**
**30 ml (2 tbls) dry sherry**
**100 g (4 oz) caster sugar**
**sprigs of rosemary or the thinly**
**peeled zest of a lemon**

Beat the cream, wines and sugar
together to form a thick froth, and
spoon into large wine glasses. Insert
the rosemary or lemon as desired,
and allow to stand in a cool place for
at least 12 hours before serving. The
resulting syllabub is one of the most
delicately flavoured, smooth and
delicious of all 17th-century dishes.

Sir Kenelm Digby: *The Closet of Sir Kenelm
Digby Opened*

*May 12th (Lord's day)*

Up, and to my chamber, to settle some accounts there, and by and by down comes my wife to me in her night-gown, and we begun calmly, that upon having money to lace her gown for second mourning, she would promise to wear white locks no more in my sight, which I, like a severe fool, thinking not enough, begun to except against, and made her fly out to very high terms and

Samuel Pepys (1633–1703)
by Sir Godfrey Kneller

cry, and in her heat told me of keeping company with Mrs. Knipp, saying, that if I would promise never to see her more—of whom she hath more reason to suspect than I had heretofore of Pembleton—she would never wear white locks more. This vexed me, but I restrained myself from saying anything, but do think never to see this woman—at least, to have her here more, but by and by I did give her money to buy lace, and she promised to wear no more white locks while I lived, and so all very good friends as ever, and I to my business, and she to dress herself. Against noon we had a coach ready for us, and she and I to White Hall, where I went to see whether Sir G. Carteret was at dinner or no, our design being to make a visit there, and I found them set down, which troubled me, for I would not then go up, but back to the coach to my wife, and she and I homeward again, and in our way bethought ourselves of going alone, she and I, to go to a French house to dinner, and so enquired out Monsieur Robins, my perriwigg-maker, who keeps an ordinary, and in an ugly street in Covent Garden, did find him at the door, and so we in; and in a moment almost had the table covered, and clean glasses, and all in the French manner, and a mess of potage first, and then a couple of pigeons a la esterve, and then a piece of boeuf-a-la-mode, all exceeding well seasoned, and to our great liking; at least it would have been anywhere else but in this bad street, and in a perriwigg-maker's house; but to see the pleasant and ready attendance that we had, and all things so desirous to please, and ingenious in the people, did take me mightily. Our dinner cost us 6s., and so my wife and I away to Islington.

Samuel Pepys (1633–1703)

# ORANGE BUTTER

R. a quarter of a Pint of cleared
juice of Oranges, a quarter of a Pint
of white wine, pare the Peel of your
Oranges thinne, steep itt in the juice
& white-wine halfe an hour, then
put in when you have taken out the
pill a little fine Sugar, to take away
the sharpnesse. Then beat the yolks
of six eggs very well, & put them into
the liquor, & sett them over the fire,
& keep itt continually stirring till
you find it almost as thick as Butter
then throw itt about the dish or
bason, & let itt stand all night, in
the morning take
itt off lightlie
with a spoon, &
serve itt as other
Butter.

**150 ml ('/4 pt) fresh orange juice,
and thinly peeled zest of the
oranges**
**150 ml ('/4 pt) white wine**
**6 egg yolks**
**30 ml (2 tbls) sugar**

Soak the zest in the orange juice and
white wine for 30 minutes to enrich
the flavour, and then remove. Beat the
egg yolks and sugar and add to the
orange juice. Pour the mixture into a
saucepan, and stir continuously over a
low heat until thick and creamy, making
sure it does not boil. Allow the butter
to cool and serve with wafers as a rich,
full-flavoured fruit dip.

*The Savile Recipe Book, 1683,* quoted in
*The Gentlewoman's Kitchen*

# SACK POSSET

*My Lord of Carlisle's Sack-possett:*
*Take a Pottle of Cream, and boil in it*
*a little whole Cinnamon, and three or*
*four flakes of Mace. To this*
*proportion of Cream put in eighteen*
*yolkes of Eggs, and eight of the whites;*
*a pint of Sack. Beat your Eggs very*
*well, and mingle them with your*
*Sack, Put in three quarters of a*
*pound of Sugar into the Wine and*
*Eggs with a Nutmeg grated, and a*
*little beaten Cinnamon; set the basin*
*on the fire with the wine and Eggs,*
*and let it be hot. Then put in the*
*Cream boyling from the fire, pour it*
*on high, but stir it not; cover it with a*
*dish, and when it is settled, strew on*
*the top a little fine Sugar mingled*
*with three grains of Ambergreece and*
*one grain of Musk and serve it up.*

**9 egg yolks**
**4 egg whites**
**275 ml (¹/₂ pt) dry sherry**
**1.5 ml (¹/₄ tsp) cinnamon**
**1.5 ml (¹/₄ tsp) ground mace**
**2.5 ml (¹/₂ tsp) grated nutmeg**
**1.1 l (2 pt) single cream**
**175 g (6 oz) sugar**

Beat together the egg yolks, egg whites, sherry and spices. Place in a large saucepan and heat gently, stirring constantly, until warm but still not thickened. Heat the cream and sugar together and, as it rises to the full boil, pour from a good height into the warm eggs and sherry mixture. Allow the posset to stand in a warm place for a few minutes, sprinkle a little sugar across its surface, and serve.

Sir Kenelm Digby: *The Closet of Sir Kenelm Digby Opened*

# MARMALADE

*To make marmelade of Lemmons or Oranges: Take ten Lemmons or Oranges and boyle them with halfe a dozen pippins, and so drawe them through a strainer, then take so much sugar as the pulp dooth weigh, and bottle it as you doe Marmelade of Quinces, and boxe it up.*

**For 900 g (2 lb) marmalade use:**
**5 large lemons or oranges**
**3 apples (Cox's pippins, for**
    **example)**
**150 ml (¹/₄ pt) water**
**about 450 g (I lb) sugar**

Cut the pointed ends off the lemons, quarter them, and take out the pips while holding them over a stainless steel pan. Peel, core, and quarter the apples, then place them in the pan with the lemons and water, cover and simmer gently until tender (about 45–60 minutes). Remove the fruit from the heat and convert it into a stiff pulp either by rubbing it through a sieve with the back of a wooden spoon, or by blending it until smooth. Weigh the pulp, transfer it into a clean saucepan with its own weight of sugar, and stir over a low heat until it boils to setting point (105°C/221°F). If it is to be stored for some time, the marmalade may be packed into glass jars and sealed in the usual way. For serving within the next day or so, it may be either spooned into small waxed paper baking cases, or spread as a 10 mm (¹/₂ in) thick slab on to a sheet of waxed paper. It can then be cut into small cubes, sprinkled with caster sugar, and eaten with a fork.

Sir Hugh Platt: *Delightes for Ladies*

# INGREDIENTS

By the opening of the 17th century, most of our present-day foodstuffs had already been introduced. The English countryside, parks and farms, were producing venison and all other kinds of game, mutton, pork, and beef, while increasing quantities of beef were also being imported from Scotland. Ever since the Union of the Crowns in 1603, great herds of black cattle had been driven south over the border, slowly working their way down to London with beasts being sold off at fairs en route. On all but the poorest tables, meat often formed some three-quarters of every meal. Much of this was freshly killed, but various techniques of salting and potting enabled it to be preserved for use throughout the winter months.

Most vegetables grown today were already known, ranging from cabbages, savoy, kale, cauliflower and broccoli to carrots, turnips, parsnips, beetroot, artichokes, onions, peas and beans. Common (or sweet), Virginian and Canadian potatoes were grown here too, but they were still regarded as a novelty. The interest in gardening which had begun in the later 16th century continued to

*Opposite:* A selection of foodstuffs enjoyed in the Stuart period

Radishes, and other salad vegetables, enjoyed increasing popularity

grow; orchards and gardens now yielded a wealth of fruit, in addition to lettuce, chicory, celery, cucumbers and radishes. The medieval suspicion of raw vegetables and fruit was slowly subsiding and salads were beginning to appear on the table with increasing frequency. In 1699 John Evelyn even published a whole book on the subject, *Acetaria: a Discourse of Sallets*, in which he suggested a dressing made of three parts olive oil, one part vinegar, lemon or orange juice, dry mustard, and mashed hard-boiled egg yolks.

New foodstuffs imported from overseas during this period included allspice or Jamaica pepper from the West Indies, cochineal from Mexico, and sago from Malaya. From the 1640s, when the English colonists in Barbados turned their land over to sugar cane, sugar became much more plentiful, leading to a great increase in the production of home-made preserves, confectionery and syrups. The most significant group of new foods, however,

'We have said how necessary it is that in the composure of a sallet, every plant should come in to bear its part, without being overpower'd by some herb of a stronger taste, so as to endanger the native sapor and virtue of the rest; but fall into their places, like the notes in music, in which there should be nothing harsh or grating: And though admitting some discords (to distinguish and illustrate the rest) striking in all the more sprightly, and sometimes gentler notes, reconcile all dissonances, and melt them into an agreeable composition.'

John Evelyn, *Acetaria: a Discourse of Sallets, 1699*

were all beverages. By the 1660s, it was possible to purchase in London: 'That excellent and by all Physitians approved China drink called by the Chineans Tcha, by other nations Tay alias Tee', 'Coffa, which is a blacke kind of drinke made of a kind of Pulse like Pease, called Coaus', which came from Arabia and Turkey, and chocolate, from the West Indies. Despite complaints that these novel drinks would damage the trade in home-grown barley and malt, in addition to making men 'as unfruitful as the deserts', they all enjoyed a popularity which has continued unabated up to the present day.

In addition to these new and exotic dishes, great strides were being made in the use of traditional home-grown produce. This was most clearly seen in bakery, where a whole host of significant developments were taking place. The 'great cakes' of the medieval period, enriched with butter, cream, eggs and sugar, heavily fruited and spiced, raised with yeast, and weighing 9 kilos or more, continued to be popular for

During the 17th century tea-drinking developed into a fashionable ritual. The ceremony would begin by unlocking the caddy where the precious leaves were stored. Then, the tea was carefully measured out into a warmed porcelain teapot before steaming hot water was poured on, and the lid replaced. It would be left to infuse for a few moments before being poured into small delicate bowls whose style and decoration reflected the Chinese origins of tea. The drink was then savoured without adding either milk or sugar. Due to its high price, tea was only enjoyed in aristocratic circles where it was prized for its medicinal qualities.

The tea drinking ceremony: *Top left:* Measuring the precious tea-leaves into the teapot; *Below left:* A maidservant pours on the hot water; *Below right:* Savouring the tea

important occasions. Now they were contained within a tinplate hoop, however, thus making them much more convenient both to bake and to serve. One new variety was the Banbury cake. Specially baked for wedding feasts, its outer layer of plain dough concealed a rich filling of dough mixed with currants. It was in this period too that the modern baked gingerbread appeared, this somewhat sticky sponge, flavoured with ginger and cinnamon, replacing the earlier solid paste of highly spiced breadcrumbs and wine.

Biscuits went through a similar transformation. The medieval biscuit had been made by dusting slices of an enriched bread roll with sugar and spices before returning them to the oven where they hardened into a kind of sweet rusk. By baking the biscuit-bread in the form of a single, light, finely-textured loaf, it changed into sponge cake. This was often entitled 'fine cake' in contemporary recipe books. Other popular varieties of biscuit were gumballs or

*Opposite:* Scene from a 17th-century London coffee house

*Below:* Designs for gumballs or jumbals

> '**Would'st thou both eat thy cake and have it?**'
>
> George Herbert,
> English poet, (1593–1633)

jumbals, where caraway-flavoured dough was worked up into knots or plaits, and Shrewsbury cakes whose rounds of shortcake could be spiced with ginger or cinnamon.

As baking skills developed throughout England, some areas acquired a reputation for their own local specialities. This was particularly true of a number of northern towns, Chorley, Eccles, Dewsbury and Halifax giving their names to distinct variations of the currant pasty.

'Blessed be he that invented pudding', wrote M Misson in the 1690s; 'Ah, what an excellent thing is an English pudding!' Savoury black and white puddings forced into animal guts had been made for generations, but the early 17th century saw the development of that great English invention, the pudding cloth. Utilising this simple device, it was possible to convert flour, milk, eggs, butter, sugar, suet, marrow and raisins etc into a whole series of hot, filling and nutritious dishes with minimal time, trouble and cost. Having securely tied the ingredients within the cloth, the pudding had only to be plunged into a boiling pot, perhaps along with the meat and vegetables, where it could simmer for hours without further attention. Varying in texture and quality from light, moist custards to substantial masses of heavily fruited oatmeal, the boiled pudding soon became a mainstay of English cookery, being adopted by all sections of society.

Further puddings or 'pudding pies' were poured into dishes and baked in the oven. Rice puddings were readily made in this way, as were whitepots, the luxurious predecessors of bread-and-butter pudding.

# EQUIPMENT

In 17th-century kitchens, activity centred around large, broad-arched fireplaces recessed into the walls, each measuring at least 2 metres wide by a metre in depth. Here great log fires supported on firedogs, or coal fires raised within elevated wrought-iron baskets, provided all the heat necessary for boiling and roasting. Boiling was one of the most economical ways of cooking – cauldrons of iron or brass suspended over the fire being employed to heat whole meals in a single operation. Joints of meat could be plunged into the boiling water together with vegetables contained in net bags, as well as puddings (either tied up in cloths or floating in wooden bowls) and remain there until thoroughly cooked. As an alternative, poultry, game or small quantities of meat could be placed in an earthenware vessel with butter, herbs and spices, then topped with a lid sealed in place with a strip of pastry, and the whole vessel immersed in the cauldron for a few hours. In this way, richly flavoured and tender dishes were produced, including jugged hare, in which the jointed animal was cooked within a jug.

*Opposite:* Cooking over an open fire using an iron cauldron

> ‘Out-did the meat, out-did the frolick wine.’
>
> Robert Herrick(1591–1674),
> *Ode to Ben Jonson*

For roasting, meat was mounted on long iron spits or ‘broaches’ supported on spit dogs or cobirons. Here it could be roasted before the fire, probably for four or five hours in the case of a large joint. For the turnspit, the youth employed to turn the spit, it was a laborious, boring and uncomfortable job, his front being roasted by the heat of the fire while his back was chilled by the cold draughts which rushed forward to fan the flames. It is not surprising that this was the first domestic process to be fully mechanised. From the early 17th century, weight-driven clockwork jacks mounted on the sides of the fireplaces were increasingly used to turn the spits at a slow and uniform rate. In some kitchens dog-power was preferred. Doctor Caius, founder of Caius College, Cambridge, stated that: ‘There is comprehended, under the curs of the coarsest kind, a certain dog in kitchen service excellent. For when any meat is to be roasted, they go into a wheel, which they turning about but with the weight of their bodies, so diligently look to their business, that no drudge or scullion can do the meat more cunningly, whom the popular sort hereupon term turnspits.'

Turning the meat was only one of the tasks involved in roasting. Even before it was secured on to the spit, game and poultry had to be cleaned and trussed, while sucking pigs required more detailed attention. Having made sure that the mouth was wedged open before rigor mortis set in, this most succulent of roasts was mounted on the spit, stuffed with bread and herbs such as sage, sewn up, and then placed before the fire. As roasting proceeded, the drops of fat issuing from the meat were caught in a long shallow dripping pan whose sloping base conducted them into a central well. From here

In this broadside of 1641, Mistress Abel fixes a chicken on the spit in her kitchen at 'The Ship', Old Fish Street, London

they could be taken up with a basting ladle and poured back over the meat, to keep it moist and tender.

For heating smaller quantities of food, saucepans were made of iron, bronze, tinned copper, or silver. As they were difficult to use over the open fires, they were supported either on a brigg, a horizontal framework bridging the topmost firebars, or on a trivet, a tall three-legged iron stand which stood in front of the fire to take advantage of the radiant heat. Alternatively, a shorter version of the trivet, called a brandreth, could hold a pan just a few inches above the gentle heat of a small fire burning on the hearth. Skillets and posnets were also used in this position, their pan-like bodies being raised on three integral legs.

In large establishments, where entertainment was provided on a lavish scale, the kitchen usually housed a stove in addition to the normal fireplace. This took the form of a long masonry bench built against the wall, usually being placed close to a window to ensure adequate ventilation. Its working

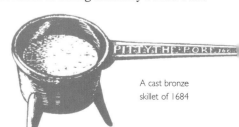

A cast bronze
skillet of 1684

One of the most ingenious culinary inventions of this period was the pressure-cooker or 'digester'. Denys Papin, a French physicist and mathematician living in London, discovered that most foodstuffs could be efficiently cooked in a totally sealed vessel, thus making considerable savings in time, fuel and flavour. To demonstrate the advantages of this method, he invited a number of fellow-members of the Royal Society to join him for a supper in April 1682, at which 'all was dressed, both fish and flesh, in digesters, by which the hardest bones were made as soft as cheese, without water or other liquor, and with less than eight ounces of coals, producing an incredible quantity of gravy, but nothing exceeded the pigeons, which tasted just as if baked in a pie, all of these being stewed in their own juice, without any addition of water save what swam about the digester'. As with so many other improvements, centuries were to pass before these advantages were fully appreciated, and pressure-cooking finally became an everyday method of preparing meat, fish and vegetables for the table.

surface was pierced by a number of iron-sheathed fire baskets, their bases being separated from open flues below by a series of closely spaced firebars. Once filled with glowing charcoal, the stove provided a clean and easily controlled heat, ideal for making sauces, preserves or many made dishes.

The only other cooking facility to be found in the 17th-century kitchen was the bee-hive oven. This was a circular domed construction, measuring perhaps a metre or more in diameter, built into the thickness of

one of the walls and entered by way of a small, square doorway. The equipment and methods used in baking bread, one of the major tasks in any household, are

clearly described in Randle Holme's *Academy of Armory* of 1688. Using a meal shovel (1), the baker first transferred a batch of flour from a large storage chest or ark into a plank-built kneading trough (2). Here it was blended with warm water, salt or spices, and yeast which had been made by dissolving a piece of old sour dough in water.

Illustrations of a baker's tools in Randle Holme's *Academy of Armory*

The soft dough was then removed from the trough using a dough scraper (3), and transferred to the brake (4), a strong table fitted with a long hinged roller with which the dough was kneaded and beaten until ready for moulding. On the moulding table (5), a long dough knife (6) was used to divide the dough so that it could be weighed and moulded into loaves or rolls. After the loaf had been cut, by running the knife around the sides, and pricked across the top with a sharp bodkin, it was stamped with the baker's name or mark so that it could be readily identified if found faulty or short in weight.

It was now ready for the oven (7). This had been fired to a high temperature by thrusting a burning bunch of gorse into its chamber, using a short pitchfork (8). When the oven was up to temperature, the fire and ashes were swept out, and the loaves slipped inside using a long-handled peel (9). Once the oven had been sealed with a slab of stone, set in place with clay or dirt from

> '**Of all smells, bread;**
> **of all tastes, salt.**'
>
> George Herbert,
> English poet, (1593–1633)

the street, the heat remaining in the masonry slowly baked the bread to perfection. Having broken away the mud which sealed the door, the oven was opened and the bread drawn out on the peel. As there was still a considerable quantity of heat left in the oven, further items of bakery, such as puddings, pasties and pies which required longer low-temperature cooking, were then inserted. If custards were being made, their blind pastry cases were now put in and filled almost to the brim with a sweet egg and milk mixture poured from a long-handled wooden custard filler (10). The door was then sealed in place again and the contents left to bake for the required time. If further baking was required, the whole process had to be repeated, reheating the oven with more gorse, cleaning out the hot embers, etc. It is not surprising that the first iron ovens which were able to provide a constant source of heat proved to be so successful when introduced in the 18th century.

Although ice cream was enjoyed in the Far East for many centuries, it was first recorded in England in the 17th century. It is thought that aristocrats making the Grand Tour brought back a recipe from Italy. Another theory claims that it originated from a special royal delicacy concocted by a French cook of Charles II which was deemed so special that only the guests at the king's table were allowed to eat it. A taste for ice cream soon developed and the cooks in the kitchens of royal and aristocratic households needed to learn new skills in order to serve it. By constructing straw-thatched ice-houses, or snow-pits, dug deep into the ground, it was now possible to keep stocks of winter ice throughout the year. When ice cream was required, blocks of ice were brought into the kitchen, broken into lumps, and packed around a small metal pail containing sweetened cream, and then perhaps flavoured with orange flower water. Having been left to freeze for a couple of hours, it was turned out on to a salver and sent up to the table, where it formed an interesting and popular addition to the banquet course.

# TABLEWARE

Up to the opening decades of the 17th century the gentry had lived within large households, usually thirty or more in number, including relations, chaplains, tutors, porters and a large number of servants. In all but the grandest houses, they all dined together in the great hall. The master and his chief guests sat at the top table, probably raised on a dais surmounted by a tall canopy, while the remainder occupied tables below, in the body of the hall. When the gentry started to spend more time in town, and more money on personal pleasures, the old-fashioned extended household proved to be an expensive encumbrance, and soon became a thing of the past.

Imitating the Elizabethan nobility, the gentry now abandoned the great hall for all but the largest social events, and began to take their meals in a completely new setting – the dining room. In older houses, the parlour, a private bed-sitting room, was often transformed into a dining room, with new decorations and furniture, while in new houses a good quality purpose-built dining room was of the greatest importance. With its walls lined with elegant timber panelling or embossed, painted and gilded Cordovan goatskin, its plaster ceiling enriched with mouldings and robustly modelled ornament, its impressive fireplace and curtained windows, the dining room provided an ideal setting in which to entertain guests, and make a powerful display of wealth and taste.

A cutaway reconstruction drawing by Philip Winton of
Hardwick Old Hall, Derbyshire, in the early 17th century

From the middle of the century, dining rooms were being furnished with a dining table, often of the oval gate-legged variety, surrounded by a matching set of chairs for the most important diners. There might also be a

> '**Strange to see how a good dinner and feasting reconciles everybody.**'
>
> Samuel Pepys (1633–1703)

long table and a set of stools for other members of the household, while livery cupboards or sideboards would be provided both to hold dishes of food and to display vessels of gold, silver or fine pottery.

When preparing the table, it was first covered with a fine linen cloth, probably woven with a damask design. Over this, the table was laid with all the required plates, salts, casters and saucers. These were made of silver or silver-gilt in the larger houses, for they provided a convenient and ostentatious means of storing one's wealth in a period where modern banking systems were still in their infancy. Much early plate was melted down during the Civil War, but from the Restoration there was a great revival in the use

> 'Fill all the glasses there, for why
> Should every creature drink but I?
> Why, man of morals, tell me why?'
>
> Abraham Cowley (1618–1667)

of silver tableware, which now appeared in a whole range of new and elegant designs. In 1670, for example, Prince Rupert purchased five dozen silver plates from Alderman Blackwell, each plate weighing $17^3/_4$ ounces at 5s 8d per ounce, the whole set costing almost £300. This gives some indication of the high costs involved in furnishing a table with good-quality silverware. Much of this domestic plate was made in London, where it found a ready market among the nobility and gentry who came up to town for the winter season, but major regional centres such as Newcastle, York, Chester, Norwich and Exeter also produced silverware of the highest standard.

*Opposite:* Brightly painted platters in the 17th-century style

Since solid silver was extremely expensive, many households used pewter as a substitute. Composed of tin, with a small percentage of lead and copper, this metal cost only 1s to 1s 2d a pound, and therefore could be used in much greater quantities by a far wider section of the community. When polished, it closely resembled silver, but it was much softer. Even a moderately hard cut with a knife would score its surface quite deeply, so that it was in need of constant maintenance, the marks received at table either burnished over, or polished out using fine abrasive sand.

This troublesome operation could be avoided by using delftware made of a light biscuit-coloured pottery covered in a smooth and glossy opaque white glaze. Having been made in England from the 1560s, it now enjoyed great popularity. Production was being centred in the London parishes of Aldgate and Southwark and, from the mid-17th century, at Brislington near Bristol. Many pieces were decorated with blue brushwork in the Chinese manner imitating Ming or 'Transitional' porcelain, while others, particularly the large 'blue-dash chargers' (so-called from the decoration around their rims), were painted with brightly coloured flowers, portraits, or pictures of Adam and Eve. English lead-glazed earthenware also made great advances from the mid-17th century, particularly in the manufacture of tableware. By the 1660s, the supremacy of the Staffordshire potters had already become fully established, their slipwares decorated in coloured liquid clays being particularly attractive. The great dishes of Thomas Toft, with their lively royal portraits or coats of arms, provided appropriately loyal images for the dining room.

In many households, wooden tableware was still in use, the square wooden trencher, with a large hollow for meat and a small hollow for salt, now being replaced by circular wooden plates or platters. Large communal drinking bowls still survived too, but from the end of Elizabeth's reign glassware had become much more

A Bellarmine jug

# THE
# LAMENTABLE
## COMPLAINTS
### OF
### NICK FROTH the Tapster, and RVLEROST the Cooke.

*Concerning the restraint lately set forth,*
*against drinking, potting, and piping on the Sab-*
*bath day, and against selling meate.*

common, appearing in the form of wine glasses, tumblers, and an excellent range of sweetmeat, jelly and syllabub glasses.

The most significant change in tableware was the introduction of the fork. Forks had been used for eating sweetmeats in royal and noble houses since the 14th century, but they only emerged as a major item of cutlery from the early 17th century, when they were popularised by Thomas Coryat. He published an account of their use in Italy in 1611, while in 1616 Ben Jonson asked:

'Forks? What be they?'
'The laudable use of forks,
Brought into custom here, as they are in Italy,
To the sparing of napkins.'

Half a century was to pass before they were generally accepted, however, but by the 1660s sets of knives and forks were being made. The knife now adopted a rounded end, in contrast to its earlier pointed form which had been necessary when it had to spear meat from the dishes.

In this broadside of 1641, the tapster and the cook complain of the new regulations which prevent them from trading on Sundays. Note the cook's 'lusty surloins of roast Beefe' turning in front of the fire

ANNO 1602

ECCE SIC BENEDICETVR HOMO.
QVI TIMET DOMINVM

# THE MEALS

At this period the day was punctuated by three main meals: breakfast, taken shortly after rising; dinner, taken at midday; and supper, taken in the early evening. The first of these was a relatively light meal by the standards of the day, probably having a selection of cold meats, bread and butter, and cakes served with tea, coffee or chocolate by the end of the century. However, then – as now – there were great contrasts in breakfast preferences, the Cromwells, for example, taking rich broth or caudle, followed by a cup of small ale with toast and sugar at mid-morning.

Unlike today's dinners, in which the frequent courses follow each other in a set sequence from soup to dessert, the 17th-century dinner was only of two, or, at most, three courses. Each course comprised a number of diverse dishes, including both sweets and savouries, so that the diner could help himself to whatever he liked in the manner of a modern buffet, thus giving each individual a much greater freedom of choice. The first course would be placed on the table in a neat, symmetrical arrangement, and include most of the

*Opposite: A Portrait of a Family saying Grace Before a Meal, 1602 by Gortzius Geldorp, (1553–1618)*

major meat dishes, together with soups which would be removed and their place taken by a further dish once everyone had been served. In the second course there would be a range of lighter meats, game and sweet dishes laid in a similar symmetrical pattern, but this division was only a general rule, leaving plenty of scope to include whatever might be available at any particular time.

The third course was composed of fruit, sweets and cheese, but the manner in which it was served changed as the century progressed. In the earlier decades, it continued the popular Elizabethan practice of banqueting; the 'banquet' in this case being an elaborate dessert course of sweetmeats, etc served either as a meal in itself or as a continuation of dinner or supper, usually set out in a separate

> The strawberry: 'Doubtless God could have made a better berry, but doubtless God never did.'
>
> Dr William Butler, 17th-century English writer

apartment. It presented an opportunity for the cooks and the gardeners to make a great show of their skills, with elaborate confections and rare fruits displayed in new and exciting ways. For important functions, cardboard galleons sailing on seas of salt could startle guests with their cannon, fired with real gunpowder, while pastry deer bled red wine when arrows were pulled from their sides.

John Evelyn gives the following colourful account of William and Mary's entertainment for the Venetian ambassadors, when 'the banquet was twelve vast chargers piled up so high that those that sat one against another could hardly see each other. Of these sweetmeats, which doubtless took some days piling up in this exquisite manner, the Ambassadors touched not, but left them to the spectators ... in a moment of time all that curious work was demolished, the confitures voided, and the tables cleared.' This appears to have been the fate of many royal banquets. Even when the Garter knights held their great dinner in the magnificent Banqueting House in Whitehall, 'the banqueting-stuff was flung around the room profusely'. In most households, however, particularly from the Restoration, the third course began to be served at the dining table, in the manner of a modern dessert.

Sage: 'Good for diseases of the liver and to make blood. A decoction of the leaves and branches of Sage made and drunk, saith Dioscorides, provokes urine and causeth the hair to become black. It stayeth the bleeding of wounds and cleaneth ulcers and sores. Three spoonsful of the juice of Sage taken fasting with a little honey arrests spitting or vomiting of blood in consumption. It is profitable for all pains in the head coming of cold rheumatic humours, as also for all pains in the joints, whether inwardly or outwardly. The juice of Sage in warm water cureth hoarseness and cough. Pliny saith it cureth stinging and biting serpents. Sage is of excellent use to help the memory, warming and quickening the senses. The juice of Sage drunk with vinegar hath been of use in the time of the plague at all times. Gargles are made with Sage, Rosemary, Honeysuckles and Plantains, boiled in wine or water with some honey or alum put thereto, to wash sore mouths and throats, as need requireth. It is very good for stitch or pains in the sides coming of wind, if the place be fomented warm with the decoction in wine and the herb also, after boiling, be laid warm thereto.'

Nicholas Culpeper (1616–54),
*A Physicall Directory*, 1649

At supper, early in the evening, only a single course was laid, but it could be made up of numerous dishes, or be extended by a banquet whenever necessary. Then, after a few hours of good conversation, music, singing or cards, accompanied by much alcohol and, perhaps, tobacco, the company would be served with a light meal to prepare them for their homeward journey or for the chill of the bedroom – Pepys, for example, having 'a good sack-posset and cold meat and sent my guests away about 10-a-clock at night'. The sack posset certainly provided the ideal close to the day. Made of eggs, wine and spices scalded with sweetened cream, spooned from the most beautifully decorated silverware, or sipped from voluminous earthenware vessels, its rich, smooth warmth and alcoholic potency soon lulled the diners into total oblivion. 'And so to bed.'

# BIBLIOGRAPHY

Anon, *The Second Book of Cookery* (London, 1641).

Anon, *A Book of Fruits & Flowers*, 1653, reprinted with an introduction by C. Anne Wilson, by Prospect Books (London, 1984).

Avery, Madam Susanne, *A Plain Plantain*, 1688 (Ditchling, Sussex, 1922).

Brears, P.C.D., *The Gentlewoman's Kitchen*, Wakefield Historical Publications (Wakefield, 1984).

Cromwell, Elizabeth (Joan), *The Court and Kitchen of Mrs Elizabeth Commonly called Joan Cromwell*, 1664, reprinted by Cambridgeshire Libraries (Cambridge, 1983).

Digby, Sir Kenelm, *The Closet of Sir Kenelm Digby Opened*, 1669 (London, 1910).

Driver, C., and Berridale-Johnson, M., *Pepys at Table*, Bell and Hyman (London, 1984).

Evelyn, John, *Acetaria: a Discourse of Sallets*, 1699, reprinted by Prospect Books (London, 1984).

Fairfax, Henry, and others, *Arcana Fairfaxiana*, mid-17th century (Newcastle, 1890).

May, Robert, *The Accomplisht Cook* (London, 1660).

Mosley, Jane, *Jane Mosley's Derbyshire Recipes 1669-1712*, Derbyshire Museums' Service (Derby, 1979).

# Bibliography

Murrel, J., *A New Booke of Cookerie*, 1615, reprinted by Da Capo Press (New York, 1972).

Platt, Sir Hugh, *Delightes for Ladies To adorne their Persons, Tables, Closets, and Distillatories with Beauties, Banquets, Perfumes and Waters*, printed by Humferey Lownes (London, 1608).

Price, Rebecca, *The Compleat Cook*, 1681, Routledge and Kegan Paul (London, 1974).

Spurling, Hilary, *Elinor Fettiplace's Receipt Book: Elizabethan Country House Cooking*, Penguin Books (Viking Salamander) (London, 1986).

W.M., *The Compleat Cook and Queen's Delight*, 1671 edn. Reprinted by Prospect Books (London, 1984).

## ACKNOWLEDGEMENTS

The publishers would like to thank Historic Haut Cuisine for cooking and presenting a number of recipes featured in this book, and James O Davies and Peter Williams for photographing them. They are also grateful for the assistance given by Derry Brabbs in supplying photographs from his collection.

The publishers would like to thank the following people and organisations listed below for permission to reproduce the photographs in this book. Every care has been taken to trace copyright holders, but any omissions will, if notified, be corrected in any future edition.

All photographs are © English Heritage. NMR with the exception of the following:
Front cover: © Christie's Images Ltd; pp9, 21, 34, 56, 60, 61, 65, 66 Derry Brabbs; p11 Bodleian Library, University of Oxford DOUCE.P.412; p14 Private collection/courtesy of The Bridgeman Art Library; pp19, 62 Mary Evans Picture Library; p50 Royal Society of Arts, London, UK/courtesy of The Bridgeman Art Library; p86 Rafael Valls Gallery, London, UK/courtesy of The Bridgeman Art Library

Line illustrations by Peter Brears

# RECICE INDEX

Other titles in this series:
Roman Cookery
Medieval Cookery
Tudor Cookery
Georgian Cookery
Victorian Cookery
Ration Book Cookery